THIS BOOK IS DEDICATED TO
THOSE WHO HOLD THESE TRUTHS
TO BE SELF-EVIDENT, THAT
ALL MEN ARE CREATED EQUAL,
AND THAT THEY ARE ENDOWED
BY THEIR CREATOR WITH
CERTAIN UNALIENABLE RIGHTS,
THAT AMONG THESE ARE LIFE,
LIBERTY, AND THE PURSUIT OF
HAPPINESS.

— EM & TR

Regnery® is a registered trademark of Salem Communications Holding Corporation

ISBN: 978-1-68451-136-5
ebook ISBN: 978-1-68451-137-2
Library of Congress Control Number: 2020936164

Published in the United States by
Regnery Publishing
A Division of Salem Media Group
www.Regnery.com

Manufactured in the United States of America

10 9 8 7 6 5 4 3

Books are available in quantity for promotional or premium use. For information on discounts and terms, please visit our website: www.Regnery.com.

DONALD
AND THE FAKE NEWS!

BY
ERIC METAXAS
& TIM RAGLIN

REGNERY
PUBLISHING
A Division of Salem Media Group

Once upon a long time ago, when people lived in caves,

there was a country called "the Land of the Free."

It was presided over by a "president" named Donald.

Donald understood that a leader should do the will

of the people he leads—and that he did!

To begin with, he drained the Swamp that had prevented

the cave people from having a say in how they were governed.

Next he helped them build a wall—

to keep out those who didn't love freedom.

And then he and the people wrote

what they called "the Constitution."

The Constitution was a sacred document

that spelled out the laws of the land!

And everyone was happy!

Well, not quite everyone.

There were some citizens

who pretended to love freedom

but actually hated it.

They called themselves "the Resistance,"

because they vowed to resist everything Donald said or did!

They met in a deep cave

and they plotted to bring the Swamp back.

That's because before Donald drained the Swamp,

they lived in it! And they had special Swampy Privileges.

But now they were just like everyone else!

Their leader was an old sorceress

whom everyone called "Madame Miss Speaker."

"Whatever Donald does," she said, "we're against it!

We must be completely NEGATIVE!

It's our only hope!"

So whatever Donald said, they contradicted it or twisted it

to make Donald seem like a bad leader!

Once, during a speech, Donald looked up and said,

"What a beautiful blue sky! Isn't that beautiful?!"

Instantly, the people in the Resistance flew into a rage!

"It's so mean of Donald to mention the blue sky!"

"What about people who live where it's raining!

Doesn't he care about them?

How can he be so thoughtless and nasty?!!"

Another time Donald saw a mother and child.

"What a cute little baby!" he said.

"How dare he refer to someone's looks!" the Resisters said.

"He's so superficial!"

"And what about people whose babies aren't so cute?"

"Doesn't Donald care about them? Donald is a monster!!!"

They said these things so often that

even some good people believed them.

Others simply got confused.

Was Donald really a bad person? He didn't seem bad...

"But why are all these people saying these things?"

"Well, maybe there is SOME truth to them..."

"Maybe we should ask Donald himself!"

So some people went and asked Donald

if these things were true.

Did he really not care about people?

Was he really a monster?

"Let me explain something," Donald said.

"When I was a builder of caves, I was very successful.

And when you're successful, you have enemies."

"And those of us who are free and love freedom

have been extremely successful!

Look at this wonderful country we've built!

So naturally, there will be some who are jealous."

"They don't like our freedom!

But they don't have the courage

to leave our country and go somewhere else.

Sad!"

"So the stories about you aren't true?"

Donald laughed. "Of course not.

Those stories are what I call Fake News!"

"What's that?"

"Fake News is when something pretends to be true, but it's not!"

"You mean it's a lie?"

"Precisely. But I say we ignore the Fake News

and just keep working hard and enjoying our freedom.

As my father used to say,

'Don't let the Turkeys get you down!'"

So the Resistance continued to spread Fake News,

but it didn't have the effect they hoped it would.

Most people still liked Donald.

And the Land of the Free continued to have

one success after another!

Meanwhile, back at the deep cave...

"We need something really big!" Madame Miss Speaker said.

"Something that will make Donald look like

a traitor to the people he represents!

That way he will be kicked out of office,

and we can take our power back!"

A cranky old man spoke up.

"It's not going to be easy!

Everyone seems to like Donald.

I saw him getting food at the delicatessen the other day,

and everyone wanted to shake his hand!

He's very popular, the big jerk!"

"You saw Donald at the deli?"

"Oh sure. He loves to mingle. A real man of the people...

ordered a Reuben sandwich—you know,

with corned beef and sauerkraut and Russian Dressing.

He gets his heavy on the Russian Dressing, with extra on the side."

This gave Madame Miss Speaker an idea.

She mumbled something to her imaginary friend.

They discussed it a bit, and then she said,

"Did you say RUSSIAN Dressing?"

"What kind of a Reuben would it be without Russian Dressing?"

the cranky old man shouted. "I had one too!

But let me be very clear—I was not copying him!

I always have a Reuben at that deli! With an egg cream and a pickle!

People want to criticize me for that?!

I apologize to nobody for that! It's delicious!"

But Madame Miss Speaker kept thinking.

"What if we say that Donald is secretly working

for the Russians who make that salad dressing!?

That everything he does is only to help them!

We can say he's just their puppet!

That he doesn't really care about the Land of the Free at all!"

"Can we do that?" someone asked.

"It's one thing to whine and complain and say negative things.

But wouldn't this be telling an out-and-out UNTRUTH?"

Madame Miss Speaker was furious.

"Do you want to win power back or don't you?"

"Let me tell you all a secret: 'There is no truth! Only power!'

And once we have power, we can control the truth forever!"

And so everyone repeated this: "There is no truth! Only power!

THERE IS NO TRUTH! ONLY POWER!"

So the next day the Resistance started spreading the rumor.

"Can you imagine that? Donald is really only working..."

"...to help those Russians sell us their salad dressing!"

"They pay him to do it!"

"And he is getting richer by the day!"

Soon everyone was talking about it.

"Isn't it horrible?"

"Our president is nothing but—
a salad dressing apparatchik!"

"Yeah! That makes him a real
no-goodnik in my opinion!"

"And everyone is saying it!
So it MUST be true!"

Finally, Madame Miss Speaker declared

it was time for a FULL investigation.

She held up a copy of the Constitution.

"We are a country of laws," she said.

"And no one is above the law!"

When people saw the Constitution,

they figured there must be something to this whole thing!

And so there was an OFFICIAL INVESTIGATION!

But it turned out to be a big waste of time and money.

And in the end, no evidence was found that

Donald was helping the Russians make salad dressing.

But Madame Miss Speaker said it didn't matter

that Donald was innocent. "This investigation will

be on Donald's permanent record forever!

SO THERE!"

Donald just rolled his eyes.

By now most people had come to see

that the whole thing was just a big silly hoax.

And the Resistance was discouraged.

Then one day Donald announced

that there must be a new presidential election!

Most people didn't feel the need for an election.

They were happy with Donald. But Donald insisted.

"If a free people are to govern themselves," he said,

"they must choose their president every four years.

It's right here in our Constitution!"

When those in the Resistance heard this, they were elated!

This was one last chance to get rid of Donald!!

So they put up their own candidate, hoping he could defeat Donald.

It was the cranky old man who saw Donald at the deli!

His name was Comrade Butt-insky.

And the Resistance dubbed him "the People's Candidate"!

"Power to the people!" he shouted. "Down with the rich!

Down with success and prosperity!

I care about you people! And I will give you free money!

Not like Dictator Donald!"

Of course, the Resistance knew that the most important part

of defeating Donald was spreading Fake News!

So they redoubled their efforts!

But Donald was not discouraged.

"A famous caveman once said:

'One word of truth outweighs the world,'

so we will continue to speak the truth!

Truth is a weapon against lies

—and it can never be defeated!"

Because there was so much Fake News while he was president,

Donald used a special way of spreading the truth.

Back in those days, to get REAL NEWS out to the people

he sometimes gave a short message to a blue bird,

who carried it straight to the people! Can you imagine?

Everyone welcomed hearing the truth for a change!

"The earth is round—not flat!"

"The sky is blue!"

"One plus one equals two!"

"Sixteen ounces make a pound!"

"E=mc squared! (I'll explain later!)"

"The truth has set us free!" they exclaimed.

"Honesty is the best policy!"

"Two wrongs don't make a right!"

"The sun rises in the east
and sets in the west!

"Fish gotta swim, birds gotta fly!"

"God loves us!"

But the Resistance couldn't take it!

The blitzkrieg of truth bombs was overwhelming!

"The ends don't justify the means!"

"Lying is wrong!"

"Capitalism works!"

"The truth always prevails in the end!"

"Four pecks make a bushel!"

They gave themselves away by howling in rage at the sky!

It accomplished nothing—so they had that going for them.

"There are four quarts to a gallon!"

"There are only two genders,
male and female!"

"Socialism works—until you run out
of other people's money!"

"Every human being is made
in God's image!"

And as the votes came in, it was clear Donald would win!

BIGLY!

When it was time to declare victory, he shouted:

"The Truth will always win out over Fake News!"

Everyone cheered!

Except those in the Resistance. They were furious!

"DOWN WITH HATE!" they cried.

But they were filled with hate when they said it!

But Madame Miss Speaker didn't say one word.

She still held the Constitution in her hands.

But she had a crazy look in her eyes

that only got crazier and crazier.

She began to twitch—and her eyes began to bulge out.

And then suddenly, she snapped!

She tore up the Constitution in her hands with everyone watching!

"Don't—you can't do that!" the people cried.

But she didn't stop.

She continued tearing it into smaller and smaller pieces!

Finally, she gathered up all the pieces in her skirt

and scattered the bits like confetti, left and right,

as she danced away like a madwoman,

all the way to the edge of a great cliff.

And then she danced...right off the cliff!

And all those who were on her side followed her!

One by one the members of the Resistance

went after her like lemmings off the cliff!

The truth had driven them all plumb loco!

When they were all gone, a great peace came over the crowd.

Then someone shouted: "The Truth will set you free!"

"Long live freedom!"

"God bless the Land of the Free!"

And so Donald and the people in the Land of the Free

continued speaking the truth.

And their freedom and prosperity increased and increased

—and it is increasing still, unto this very day!

ERIC METAXAS

ERIC METAXAS has written over thirty children's books, including the bestsellers *Squanto and the Miracle of Thanksgiving* and *It's Time to Sleep, My Love,* illustrated by Nancy Tillman. He has also been a writer for *VeggieTales*.

Since editing the *Yale Record*, the nation's oldest college humor magazine, Eric's humor has appeared in *The New Yorker* and *The Atlantic*. Woody Allen has called these pieces "quite funny." Eric wrote a full-length book parody of the Ripley's "Believe It or Not" books, titled *Don't You Believe It!*, prompting novelist Mark Helprin to call him "the thinking man's Gary Larson (*The Far Side*)."

Metaxas is the bestselling author of *Bonhoeffer: Pastor, Martyr, Prophet, Spy* and many other books, including *Martin Luther, If You Can Keep It, Miracles, Seven Women, Seven Men,* and *Amazing Grace*. His books have been translated into more than twenty-five languages.

He is the host of the *Eric Metaxas Show*, a nationally syndicated radio program heard on more than 300 stations around the US, featuring in-depth interviews with a wide variety of guests.

Metaxas was the keynote speaker at the 2012 National Prayer Breakfast in Washington, D.C., an event attended by the president and first lady, the vice president, members of Congress, and other US and world leaders.

ABC News has called him a "photogenic, witty ambassador for faith in public life," and *The Indianapolis Star* described him as "a Protestant version of William F. Buckley." Metaxas's *Wall Street Journal* op-ed, "Science Increasingly Makes the Case for God," is the most popular and shared piece in the history of the *Journal*.

Metaxas has been featured as a cultural commentator on CNN, MSNBC, and Fox News programs and has been interviewed about his work on the *Today Show, Fox and Friends, The History Channel*, and C-SPAN. He has been featured on many radio programs, including NPR's *Morning Edition* and *Talk of the Nation*, as well as *The Hugh Hewitt Show, The Dennis Prager Show,* and *The Michael Medved Show*.

Metaxas is a Senior Fellow at the King's College in New York City. He lives in Manhattan with his wife and daughter.

TIM RAGLIN

TIM RAGLIN was born and raised in Independence, Kansas, and earned a degree from Washington University's School of Fine Arts in St. Louis. He then immediately launched into the world of freelance illustration, first in St. Louis, then in New York.

Raglin has illustrated many children's picture books, the most popular being *Deputy Dan* and the *Five Funny Frights* series, each having sold over two million copies. He has also worked with Rabbit Ears Productions, a children's video company, and illustrated several of Rudyard Kipling's *Just So Stories*, including the Grammy Award-winning *The Elephant's Child*. Raglin also illustrated and directed his own version of *Pecos Bill*, which won both a Grammy Award for Best Children's Recording and a Parent's Choice Classic Award. Tim served as the creative director of Rabbit Ears until 1991.

He has since illustrated a number of children's picture books, including *The Thirteen Days of Halloween*, *The Wolf Who Cried Boy*, *Twelfth Night*, and *Go Track a Yak!*. But Raglin's chief focus has been his work as the publisher of several of his own picture books, including *Uncle Mugsy* and *The Terrible Twins of Christmas*, which received a Silver Medal from the New York Society of Illustrators. He also published *The Birthday ABC*, which was chosen as an American Library Association "Pick of the List" book in 1995. He is currently working on several new picture books, which he plans to publish under his own imprint, the first of which will be *The Curse of Catunkhamun*.

Raglin has had a number of books chosen to appear in The Original Art Show: The Best in Children's Books, as well as the New York Society's Annual Show. He lives in Independence, Kansas.